To Barbara,
  I hope the Churchill book
gives you much enjoyment.
    Best wishes,
      and Happy Birthday!

Robert R. Taylor
October 23, 1998

The Edge of the Arctic

CHURCHILL AND THE HUDSON BAY LOWLANDS

Photography and Text by Robert R. Taylor
Windermere House Publishing

Published by

Windermere House Publishing

944 Windermere Avenue

Winnipeg, Manitoba

R3T 1A1

ISBN. 1-55056-185-5

First Edition

Copyright 1992 - Robert R. Taylor

Book design by Steve Penner

Printed and bound in Canada

by DWFriesen

Altona, Manitoba, Canada

R0G 0B0

Title page -
Fragmented ice contrasts with the shoreline rocks near Cape Merry.

▶ *Green lichens cling to a background of Blue Quartzite forming a fascinating pattern on the aged rocks.*

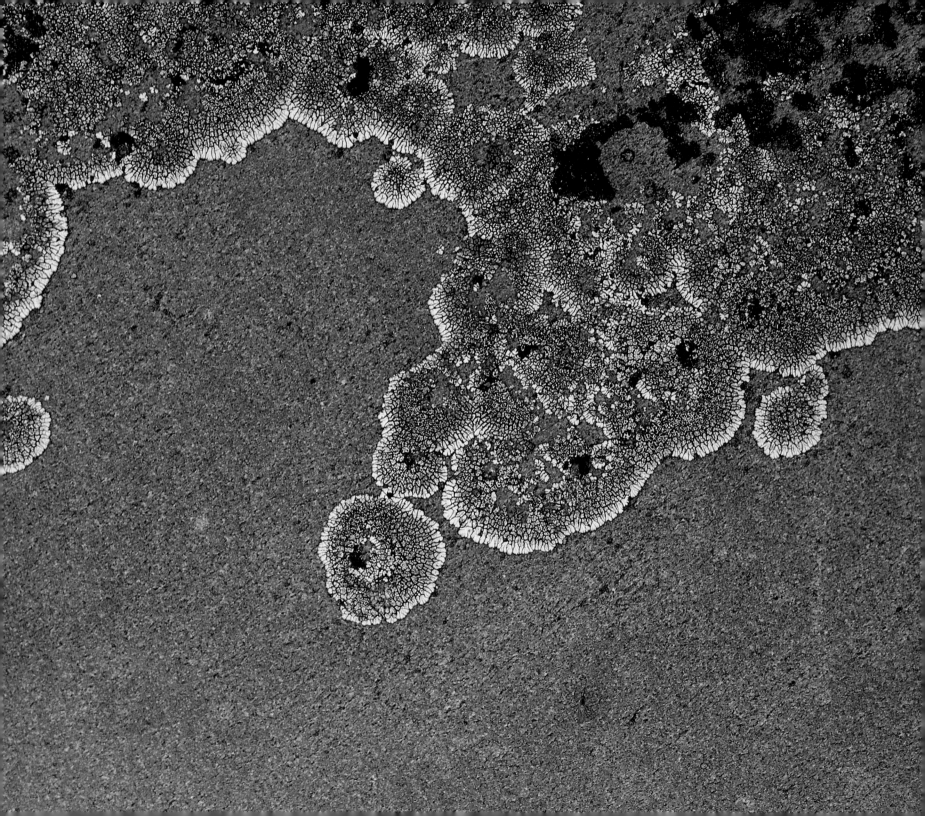

The beautiful flowers of the tiny Alpine Azalea shrub
may be found on dry peat areas in late June.

Dedication

*I would like to dedicate
this book to
my family and friends
who have always been
supportive and encouraging.*

Acknowledgements

I have made many good friends and acquaintances during my visits to Churchill. Among them are Bonnie Chartier, Churchill's resident birding authority, with whom I have spent many enjoyable days observing the local birds. Al Chartier, who pioneered the Polar Bear tours in the mid-seventies and generously shared those early adventures with me.

Bob and Pat Penwarden were very supportive on my first major photography excursion to Churchill and they have become valued friends. Doug and Helen Webber have always been encouraging and helpful since my first arrival at the Churchill airport.

My thanks to Bill Ericksen, whose reliable logistical assistance made it possible to conduct my workshops at the Northern Studies Centre and to get my field work accomplished. Dr. Fred Cooke, manager of the Snow Goose research project at LaPerouse Bay, made me welcome at the "goose camp" and often shared his expertise in science.

The late Keith Rawlings, who loved the north, was always full of ideas and encouragement to promote Churchill and my work. Penny Rawlings has continued the fine traditions of The Arctic Trading Company and has been a supportive friend.

Jim and Rita Macleod, former owners of the Arctic Inn, extended their hospitality to an appreciative nature photographer and they created a lifelong friendship.

The contribution made to this book by David G. Friesen and his professional staff at DW Friesen is immeasurable. In particular, my appreciation goes to Steve Penner, who designed this book and helped with the difficult selection of photographs.

There are many others who have helped me at Churchill over the years. They are too numerous to mention by name, but they have all been important to me and they have all been genuinely appreciated. My heartfelt thanks to all of you.

Introduction

A love affair with the north starts innocently enough. One day you find yourself looking out upon a vast expanse of land with endless sky above; the air is fresh and cool; and you know that here it is possible to feel a sense of "oneness" with the earth.

Bedrock, exposed to the elements, provides a foundation upon which volumes of glacial history and geological complexities are written. Add to this a vast array of plants, numerous birds, and a selection of unique mammals and the summer arctic captivates a willing visitor.

Each new horizon yields observations enough to occupy the discerning eye and inquisitive mind in limitless fashion. The presence of the Arctic marine habitat of Hudson Bay with its Beluga Whales, Seals, and Polar Bears enhances the appeal of this region. All ingredients combine to produce a rich dynamic ecosystem which is unique and attractive.

Within these pages is a sampling of the beautiful and varied subjects to be found in the Churchill region. I hope that the photographs fill you with memories of your excursion or will inspire you to visit this fascinating area and see it first-hand.

Preceeding page -
The Ross' Gull usually nests on a low hummock in a tundra pond or other wet spot. This very rare bird has attracted many birders to Churchill.

◀ *A spring evening on the shore of Hudson Bay is a special experience for those who seek peace and tranquility.*

Foreword

 T he Edge of the Arctic; it's a fitting description for the Hudson Bay Lowlands for it is here that the forest gives way to the open spaces of the tundra. This landscape is a unique mix of boreal forest, bedrock of the Canadian Shield, gravel eskers, old beach lines, muskeg, and marine coastline.

It is the diversity of habitat which makes the Churchill region so attractive to the numerous birds that come to nest and to feed while enroute to more distant breeding grounds. An abundance of tundra ponds and small lakes interspersed with the sedge meadows, bogs, and ridges makes the region ideal for the nesting of waterfowl and shorebirds.

In spring and early summer the haunting calls of Arctic Loons, Old-Squaws, and Common Eiders greet the ears. Overhead, spectacular aerial courtships are performed by Hudsonian Godwits, Whimbrels, Stilt Sandpipers, Common Snipes, Golden Plovers, and others. Unexpected bird visitors arrive at Churchill regularly. There are records of such species as Scissor-tailed Flycatcher, Varied Thrush, and Mountain Bluebird, which have ventured far beyond their normal range. Most notable of these rarities is the Ross' Gull, whose homeland is the Siberian region of Russia. They have nested regularly at Churchill since 1980.

The most famous inhabitant of the Hudson Bay region is the Polar Bear. Churchill is known worldwide for the bears and is proudly touted as the "Polar Bear Capital of the World". The bears gather along the shoreline in October and early November to await freeze-up so that they can move out onto the bay to hunt seals.

In the spring and summer, Bearded and Ringed Seals can be seen resting on the ice or swimming in the waters of Hudson Bay. By mid-June, as the ice pans break up or melt away, Beluga Whales make their way to the estuary of the Churchill River. Here they provide opportunities to view them at close range as they feed in the shallow waters.

There are other mammals, such as Arctic Fox, Red Fox, Wolf, Caribou, Short-tailed Weasel, and Collared Lemming, which inhabit the area but are less often seen.

The diversity of habitat offers a wide variety of plant species, about three-hundred in all. They range from delicate orchids to leathery-leaved heath plants to shrubs and trees. There is Labrador Tea, Dwarf Birch, Purple Saxifrage, Rhododendron, Bearberry, and White Spruce to name but a few. Several species of willow have been identified and many sedges. The colours of autumn are spectacular and berries are found in profusion.

Winter arrives early as the sun angles lower to the south. By mid-October there is usually a light snow cover. Snow crystals are moved around by the northern winds and behind each obstacle, however small, gracefully sculptured snowdrifts are formed. The whiteness is tinted with the blues and magentas of the low sun and darkening sky. Overhead, the Aurora Borealis dances and glows as the long silent winter begins.

Relax and Enjoy

A good book is meant to be thoroughly enjoyed. Take some time occasionally, put on some soft music, sink into your favourite chair, and let the photographs carry you off to the far north.

Let your imagination work as you relax and study the fine details. Appreciate the quality and direction of the light in each photograph. Visualize yourself as a part of the scene.

Imagine standing on the shore of Hudson Bay with a cool breeze coming off the vast expanse of sculptured ice. Pretend that you are standing ankle deep in ice-water in a flooded sedge meadow, while various shorebirds sing and display overhead. See an intricate world of compact plants, insects, and surface details as you lie on the tundra or the bedrock.

Use this book as a means to transport you to the land of the Polar Bear. Don't hide it away on a bookshelf. Use it well.

Polar Bears spend considerable time just taking it easy. This particular individual seems not to have a care in the world.

The tundra ground cover varies considerably according to the soil type,
wetness, and dominant species of plants for the conditions.

Tundra Summer

Beyond the treeline
lies a rugged land
of inspiring beauty.

In spring the tundra comes to life
welcoming the visitor
who cares to take an interest.

Its frozen surface,
unlocked briefly by the summer sun,
nourishes tenacious flora.

Accents of colour
emerge from dormant roots
in glorious, brief display.

The warmth of summer soon slips away
and the reds, yellows, and browns
of autumn are revealed.

Shortening days lose their grip
and winter again
takes control over the land.

▲ *The jewelled edge of shorebound ice glows beneath the springtime sun.*

▶ *Glacial striations are evident in the bedrock as the low sun emphasizes surface textures with long shadows.*

◄ *Many years of wave action and tumbling have rounded fragments of rock into the pebbles that are found along the Hudson Bay shore.*

► *Peaceful evenings may be spent admiring the sunset beyond the broken ice pans of the bay.*

Fort Prince of Wales, on the west side of the Churchill River, was constructed in the mid 1700's. It took thirty-eight years to complete.

*Imagine surviving a long winter within these stone walls. A misty
spring day and the anticipation of summer would be a welcomed relief.*

▲   *The town of Churchill has undergone many changes throughout its brief history. An aerial perspective from the east shows its present composition with the Churchill River beyond.*

▶   *Golden grain may be found at the end of this rainbow. Ships from around the world have come to the Churchill seaport to load their holds with this precious Canadian commodity.*

◀ *On July 1, 1767, the British explorer Samuel Hearne inscribed his name in the rock at Sloop's Cove to the south of Fort Prince of Wales. Yesterday's graffiti has become today's history.*

▶ *The rusting hull of the freighter "Ithaca" stands in silent memory of an ill-fated departure from Churchill. Stranded on the tidal flats in Bird Cove, it has now become a landmark.*

▲ *Each summer, large numbers of Beluga Whales visit the estuary of the Churchill River to feed and to moult. Beluga-watching tours offer intimate observations of these magnificent mammals.*
▶ *As spring unlocks the frozen expanse of Hudson Bay, huge masses of ice float and churn in the dynamics of the tides and the winds.*

▲ An endless array of forms and textures are presented in the ice along the coast as the spring break-up occurs in June and early July.
▶ Tide-stranded ice sculptures provide a wondrous opportunity for a cautious venture onto the "flats" at low tide.

Old-squaws return early to the tundra to await a new season of nesting and the raising of a family. Their courtship calls are one of the characteristic tundra sounds.

The Hudson Bay lowlands are interspersed with shallow ponds, muskeg, and dry ridges. This diversity of habitat makes it suitable for nesting to many species, and large numbers of birds.

In some years large numbers of migrating Ruddy Turnstones pass through Churchill
and pause for a time to rest and feed on their long journey to the Arctic islands.

Canada Geese and Lesser Snow Geese return each spring to nest in the lowlands. The Snow Geese usually nest in colonies at LaPérouse Bay but the Canada Geese disperse widely throughout the region.

◀ *Many species of willow have been identified in the Churchill area. In early June their catkins explode in a glorious tribute to spring.*

▶ *Some of the willows are low-growing, spreading out over the rocky surface or mingling with other vegetation in boggy areas. Each is unique and beautiful.*

◀ *The male Willow Ptarmigan retains his white body plumage long after the female has turned completely brown. This helps him to distract intruders into the nesting territory while she remains hidden on the nest.*

▶ *In years of an adequate vole or lemming supply, Short-eared Owls may be seen frequently. Their nest is usually concealed among the willows but occasionally they will choose an open site.*

◄ *Two species of Labrador Tea occur here. This Arctic variety is short with very narrow, leathery leaves. It grows mostly in boggy places.*

► *Purple Saxifrage is one of the earliest blooming plants, exhibiting its flowers in mid-June. Usually it grows in gravelly areas in tight clumps to prevent moisture loss from the frequent winds.*

▲ Whimbrels (*Hudsonian Curlew*) return in small flocks but soon spread out over the tundra to establish nesting territories.

▶ *The rounded forms of Blue Quartzite bedrock are the result of centuries of weathering and the grinding effects of ancient glaciers.*

Ross' Gulls began nesting near Churchill in 1980 and have continued to do so in small numbers. Their homeland is the Siberian region of Russia but a few of these circumpolar wanderers have found conditions to their liking here in Canada.

On a placid tundra lake an Arctic Tern takes an evening rest from its feeding activities and nesting duties. In the fall they embark on one of the longest migrations of any species in the world only to return to the exact same location the following spring.

▲ *The showy flowers of the Lapland Rose-Bay (Rhododendron) dominate the scene in mid-June, covering tundra ridges and damp areas.*
▶ *Moisture from the spring rains, melting snow, and grey foggy days help the tundra to come to life after a long dormant winter.*

▲   *A female Common Eider flattens herself on the nest to avoid detection and to protect her eggs.*
▶   *The beautiful Arctic Loon selects its nest site to allow easy access to the water when departing or coming onto the nest.*

Stilt Sandpipers are not common but are present in some numbers. During their aerial courtship flights the characteristic "hee-haw" call makes them easy to identify. The eggs are well camouflaged for their usually open nest sites.

About to settle upon her precious clutch, a Whimbrel takes a cautious look around. When pressed to the ground she all but disappears amid the varied cover of plants.

▲ *This stray Canada Goose gosling constantly called for its parents yet continued to feed actively upon the flowers of Bog-Rosemary.*
▶ *Within the treeline there are myriads of shallow ponds. Because the water is filtered through bog soils and vegetation it is usually crystal clear.*

▲ *The Semi-palmated Plover typically nests in gravelly areas. The speckled eggs, usually four, blend in perfectly with the surroundings.*

▶ *The Golden Plover's colouration makes them easily visible when standing. However, when they sit on the nest their mottled back becomes one with the tundra.*

The long, slightly upcurved bill of the Hudsonian Godwit is ideally suited to probing in the mud for its food. Nesting Godwits are quite secretive but when the hatchlings begin to wander throughout the bogs they will vigorously scold any perceived threat to their offspring.

It seems strange to see a long-legged wading bird perched atop a tree but it is not unusual for the Lesser Yellowlegs to do so during the nesting period. From such a vantage point they can watch and object to any interloper.

◄ *In the evening light upon Cape Merry it would be intriguing to ponder where this pebble originated and what forces brought it to this place. Peaceful evenings are made for just that sort of thing and the bedrock is a perfect place to sit and think.*

▶ *A layer of mist hangs over the ponds and partially obscures the sun. Weathered spruce trees add a unique dimension to this moody tundra scene.*

◄ *A tenacious willow gleans enough nourishment from a bit of soil in a rock fracture to sustain it for many years. It could take fifty years to grow a stalk only one-half inch in diameter.*

▶ *Most of the exposed rocks are covered with lichens of one kind or another. Displays of bright orange lichens are particularly good near Cape Merry.*

The Twin Lakes hill is one of the few high points of land to the east of Churchill. It is well worth a visit just for the chance to look out over miles of tundra landscape.

Sit quietly by a tranquil pond for a while and you will probably be rewarded by a look into the private lives of some of the local birds. You will also enjoy a variety of their songs if you tune your ears to them.

*Flame-Coloured
Lousewort stands tall
and bright in contrast to
its surroundings even
though it may be only
two or three inches high.*

The Common Butterwort has a basal rosette of sticky leaves which can trap and digest small insects. The mosquito may also help the plant by carrying pollen from one flower to another.

◀ *A pinch of soil supports this Sea-Shore Chamomile. The surrounding rock emphasizes this plant's ability to flourish under harsh conditions.*

▶ *In the latter part of July, Arnica and Hedysarum produce brilliant displays of flowers in sand and gravel areas.*

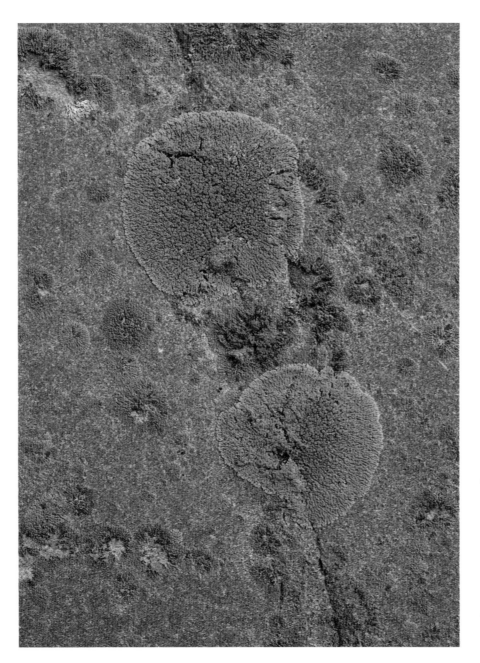

◀ *Orange Lichens offer some of the most fascinating designs for the discerning eye. Close inspection reveals an intricate network of patterns, textures, and colours.*

▶ *The fresh green of a spruce bough offers a fine complement to the variety of lichens upon the rocks beneath.*

Collared Lemmings fluctuate considerably in numbers over the years. When plentiful they attract many predators who contribute to a population downfall that may take several years to rebuild.

A familiar combination of elements in the Churchill region is that of boulders, bedrock, and weather-beaten trees. It is a harsh environment and many scenes attest to that.

Oxidation of minerals in the bedrock produces many beautiful colours and designs. There is much to satisfy the artist's eye in a place such as this. The points of land near Bird Cove are especially rich in such compositions.

Rhythmic lines in the bedrock at Halfway Point emphasize the beauty which can be found in even the most basic of subjects.

In a multi-image portrayal of the setting sun, the orange sphere disappears behind the Hudson Bay horizon even on the longest day of the year. After only about four hours it emerges a few degrees to the east.

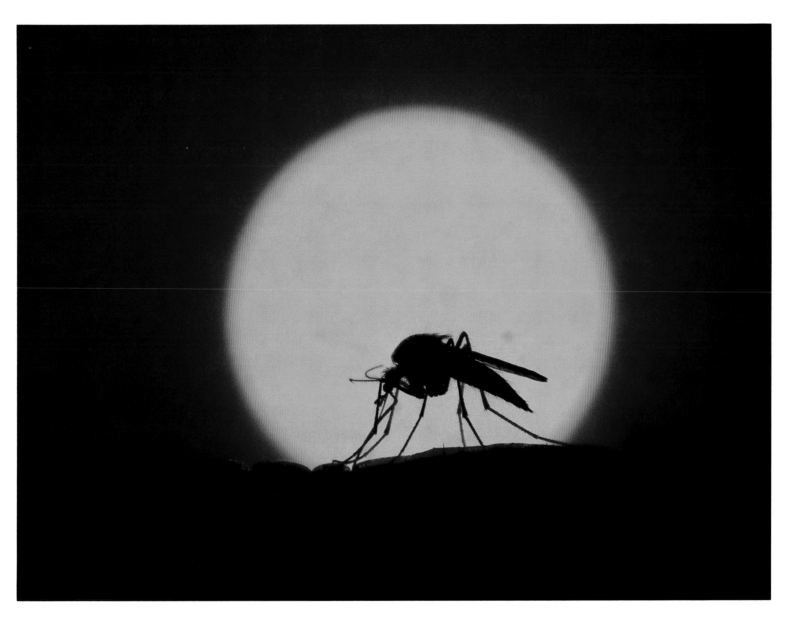

On warm summer days mosquitoes can be numerous.
Silhouetted by the setting sun this one seems larger than life.

▲ *Light plays an important role in the appreciation of the landscape. Varying in angle, colour, and brilliance, it offers unlimited combinations.*

▶ *A reddish glow illuminates the northern horizon at midnight on the summer solstice.*

▲ *Blue light reflected from the sky and orange light from the low sun combine to wash this scene in pleasant hues.*

▶ *One-sided trees, known as the "Krumholz" effect, are fashioned by the prevailing winds. Ice crystals carried by the winter winds wear down any new growth on the windward side. Dehydration on that side inhibits branch development in the short growing season.*

Knight's Hill is a major landmark to the east of Churchill. About sixty feet in height, it looms above the surrounding land and slopes off gradually to the south.

Autumn arrives in this region in late August or early September. The tundra leaves are spectacular as they exhibit their brilliant red, yellow, and orange colours.

Crimson leaves of Bearberry carpet the ground in one glorious display before they are blanketed in snow for the coming winter.

The colours of autumn are revealed when green chlorophyll production ceases at the end of the summer. This stunning display can last from a few days to a few weeks depending on the severity of the weather.

▲ *Willow Ptarmigan blend with the fall colours, but will soon turn white to help conceal them from predators on the snow-covered ground.*
▶ *There is a freshness in the air and a warmth in the scene that makes one glad to be alive and standing in this treasured place.*

▲ *Northern Lights are an awesome spectacle. They compel us to watch as they dance across the sky. The Big Dipper hangs in the sky beyond.*

▶ *Like a huge gossamer curtain, the Aurora floats above the earth in a dynamic display.*

▲ *Rock Ptarmigan migrate south to winter in the Churchill latitudes. Their summer range is considerably farther north.*

▶ *Goose Creek originates in the muskeg southeast of Churchill. As it passes through a series of tundra lakes its volume swells to make it a major feature of the landscape.*

The Arctic Fox will often curl up in the shelter of a large boulder to take a needed rest. The thick insulating fur enables them to withstand the harsh winter climate.

Following its nose an Arctic Fox will travel many miles in a day in search of food. They eat lemmings, ptarmigan, and just about anything else that they can glean from the land. Often they will hang around Polar Bears to try to scavenge a few leftover morsels from the bear's dinner.

▲ *Though powerful and potentially dangerous, young bears can be a captivating source of amusement with their comical antics.*

▶ *Icy waters are of no concern to the well-insulated cubs as they frolic and taunt each other.*

An ethereal fog surrounds a placid bear amid the willows at Bird Cove. Much of their time is spent conserving energy when food is not readily available.

Self-entertainment is not unusual for a Polar Bear. They will often play with things that they encounter during their travels, even a chunk of ice or a clump of willows.

As winter approaches the bears move to the Hudson Bay coast from their summer denning areas inland. Near the shores of the bay they will await "freeze-up" so that they can venture out onto the ice to hunt for seals.

Polar Bear cubs are carefully attended by their mothers. Though the sow may appear casual at times she is always alert to the threat from other bears, particularly larger males.

▲ *In a tender moment a sow bear reclines to nurse her cubs, a sight not often witnessed by those who come to see the Polar Bears at Churchill.*

▶ *Afternoon light reflects from newly formed ice at Gordon Point. The cubs explore the coastline with their mother, stopping frequently to rest.*

Sparring is a regular activity of bears of similar size when they congregate along the coast.
Rarely is any damage inflicted, but they do expend a lot of energy in their tests of strength.

Polar Bears put on a great show at times for observers who come to view these superb animals. They are always fascinating, especially when interacting with each other.

A ball of bears. After a period of jostling, rolling, and trying to get the best of each other, the bears will often lie down close together to rest.

The power of these large male bears is readily evident as they wrestle in the fresh snow. While on their hind legs they may stand more than eight feet tall.

▲ *Backlighted by the sun, the long guard hairs of the bear's coat glow brightly. These hairs are transparent and act much like fibre-optics to conduct light to the dark skin beneath the insulating woolly layer of fur. Thus it has a warming effect on the bear.*
▶ *During the freezing period the tides still have an effect on the bay. Receding tides can cause newly formed ice to coat the boulders of the shallow coves creating a unique backdrop for these wandering bears.*

▲ *Traversing the frozen waters of a coastal pond with the treeline off in the background, a cub dutifully follows its mother.*

▶ *Snow crystals are carried about by the Arctic winds. Accented by the low sun the snowdrifts present the qualities of great works of art.*

▲ *"Sundogs" are the result of light from the sun refracting and reflecting off ice crystals suspended in the air. They are a spectacular phenomenon usually seen on very cold days.*

▶ *Even at night the landscape can be captivating as the full moon rises beyond an isolated clump of weathered spruce. In silent splendor a long winter night begins.*

Polar Bear

White upon white,
You magnificent beast,
Amphibious master of the Arctic seas.
Ursus maritimus, Polar Bear,
Following scents
That drift on the constant wind.
At rest, you take on
The likeness of a snowdrift;
On the move,
The phantom fluid gait
Of blowing snow.